PEACE
MEDITATION
BOOK

Heavenly Father,

A prayer for Hope, Peace and encouragement
In the lives of all who read these pages.
A-men.

Faye Roots

Published in the United States of America

ISBN 978-1-970703-02-3 (SC)

ISBN 978-1-970703-03-0 (HC)

ISBN 978-1-970703-04-7 (Ebook)

For Book Rights Adaption and other Rights Permission.

Call us at toll-free **601-914-6178**.

Table of Contents

THE SURPRISE OF PEACE

Restoration of Messiah's Kingdom

The leopard shall lie down with the young goat, and the calf and the young fatling together

- Isaiah 11:6(a) NKJ -

The sound of animals fighting continued as they circled the house in heated conflict. Our son had rescued a Kelpie puppy from a drought ravaged property in central Queensland. Australian Kelpies are bred to be working dogs. This addition to our home was energetic, fast and full of mischief. The cat hated the invasion of her territory. The hissing, scratching, barking mayhem was nerve-wracking.

I wanted a quiet prayer time. I sat at the table with my bible and began to pray. I switched on a worship CD beside me. The words of a song softly filled the room. *'He is the Lamb of God – blessed sacrifice. Alpha and Omega the great I AM – the great I AM is He.'*

I heard a scuffle. The puppy came into the room and sat on my foot. The music continued and I prayed. The cat came and quietly lay down beside the pup.

For the next half-hour, the profound Presence and Peace of God filled my home. It was very special.

Prayer:

Thank You Lord,

In this world of conflicts, noise and stress You still surprise by Your Peace and the Promise of Your eternal Kingdom. We remember and ask for all, in conflict, who need this inner Peace, today.

A-men.

MEDITATIVE THOUGHT

Sometimes we need to push through our circumstance to have this quiet fellowship time with God.

Just rescued puppy Kel

Conflict!!

Mature cat – Frangi

HE SPOKE *P*EACE

Psalm 23

'I am the Good Shepherd. My sheep hear My voice'

- John 10:27 N.K.J. -

'This has been an outstanding result.' The throat surgeon's voice lingered in my mind as I settled down to sleep. I was back in my hospital room after an operation.

A few minutes later I knew something was wrong. My throat felt swollen and a bleeding lump was forming on my neck. I pressed the emergency button. Within moments the room was filled with medical staff. A nurse compressed my neck and held on with both hands.

"PEACE!" The one word came with startling clarity as I knew an overwhelming feeling of calm and well-being washing over me. *'Yea, though I walk through the valley of the shadow of death You are with me.' The words from the 23rd Psalm were alive in my mind.*

The problem – a small cut in a neck vein opened by throat swelling – was repaired. I recovered well in hospital and came home healed and restored. Thanks to God and the wonderful medical team. There was no natural explanation for the extraordinary calm and peace we all knew during the medical emergency.

My only truthful response could be 'It was God'. I also knew many people were praying and these prayers were a comforting reality even before the incident.

Father,

Thank You for the times you bring us this inexplicable surety of your Presence, in the midst, of unexpected crisis.

MEDITATIVE THOUGHT

Prayer for others may be our most important ministry this day.

He leads me beside the still, still waters

RESTRAINED BUT NEVER $\mathcal{D}$EFEATED

*These things I have spoken to you that in ME you may have peace.
In the world you will have tribulations but be of good cheer, I have
overcome the world.*

- John 16:33 (N.K.J.) –

The handbrake of my car was jammed! Exercising all my strength I couldn't release it. My husband had parked the vehicle on a lay-by beside the steep, rocky, winding, hill climb to our house on the ridge. *'Looks like I'll have to walk!'*

Hot, tired and furiously grumpy, I began to stomp up the rough road. It was not far but steep and I had several parcels.

A gentle thought came into my mind. *'You'll find this a lot easier if you calm down.'*

I returned to the car and with handbrake still on reversed it very gently further under tree shade. Then I prayed. 'Lord, please give me Your Peace and Strength to walk in serenity and without stress. A- men'. A gentle peace like a breeze came over me. I grabbed parcels and my knee brushed the handbrake as I left the car. There was a loud 'click'. I returned, started the engine and now, the brake released easily. I travelled up that hill joyfully and even laughing.

The spiritual implications in the incident were powerfully real to me. In life, circumstances – illness, sudden changes, pressures of various kinds - appear to restrain or keep us confined or trapped in the problem. A prayer of 'connection' to Christ will bring His Peace, His Strength, His Will into the circumstances.

Trials of life will never defeat us when we have the certainty of Christ with us on the journey.

This is His Gift of personal relationship – Immanuel (God is **with** us) Matt. 1:23. Christ **in** us – the hope of Glory. (Col 1:27b).

Prayer:

Thank You Lord, for Your Presence in and through all life problems.
We remember people trapped in distressing circumstances.

THE HILL TO THE HOUSE – GENTLE BUT EVER CLIMBING

MEDITATIVE THOUGHT

Sometimes the solution only comes when we pray **not** for resolution, but, for His Peace **in** the problem.

THE HIDDEN ℛEVEALED

But God has revealed them (things God has prepared for those who love Him) through His Spirit. For the Spirit searches all things, yes, the deep things of God.

- 1 Corinthians 2:10 (NKJ) –

I really loved my mother-in-law. My husband is her only child. I always felt like her daughter.

She lost a baby due to inadequate wartime antenatal care and had continuing health problems. She was never bitter or angry. She sowed love to my generation. Her grandchildren have reaped a rich heritage from the seeds of self-esteem, appreciation and courage she sowed in their lives.

When she died I felt the loss keenly. Our whole family was the poorer for her passing. My grief was highened by uncertainty about her standing with God. She believed she would go to a better place and respected the strong faith that David and I share. She never openly spoke of her own but was reverential always in her attitude to Jesus Christ.

She had particularly asked my father-in-law to give me a delicate French porcelain ornament. It is an exquisite figurine of a small boy pushing a barrow of flowers.

'O God' the cry of my heart 'This is not much to remember her by.'

The inside of the barrow was black with age and grime. Verdi grease covered the base. I decided to clean it out. Slowly and carefully I cleaned. Suddenly loose in my hand was a piece of jewellery - a simple plain, golden cross.

I held it up to the light - this symbol of the greatest love ever shown - and felt swamped by an assurance of the Grace and Love of God in her life. My heart was at peace.

Prayer: Father help us this day to be sowers of love, beauty and hope to a needing world. In Jesus' Name A-men.

MEDITATIVE THOUGHT

Hope restored.

A simple cross in the bottom of wheel barrow was a reminder of Christ's suffering sacrifice, great Love and risen Glory.

NORMAL LIFE – SIMPLY BEING AS *Jesus*

For in Him we live and move and have our being.

- Acts 17:28a –

The pedestrian traffic light changed to green. I began to run. Why? The thought calmed my haste. I walked on slowly and then waited patiently for the next light change.

A woman stopped beside me. She too had slowed her pace and missed the light. I smiled at her. 'Why do we run? What's the hurry?

She laughed. 'I don't know but I always do.'

We waited, then walked on in silence. 'Are you going this way?' She pointed. 'Perhaps we could walk together.'

I smiled and nodded. We walked on again without speaking.

'I've just been diagnosed with dementia.' Her words cut through my thoughts like a knife.

What followed can only be described as 'God moments'

I reached out and touched her shoulder. 'I'm so sorry' was all I said.

In that street with people moving around us something supernatural happened.

She asked 'Are you a Christian?'

I answered 'Yes'. Other words began to flow. I told her about relationship with God and the importance of being 'connected' to the Divine Shepherd. I also spoke about the possibilities in Him that defy human reasoning.

I shared about my friend's faith journey which has defied all her doctor's forecasts.

We parted. Her face was glowing. 'Thank you. Oh thank you.' She said. Thank YOU, my Lord! A prayer from my heart.

Each day now I find her face comes to me and she is part of my daily prayer-time.

Prayer Focus: People who have received a life-changing and threatening diagnosis.

MEDITATIVE THOUGHT

A touch of Gentle Peace brings Hope into lives disturbed by unease or anxiety.

UNSEEN PROTECTOR

The Lord will deliver me from every evil work and preserve me for His heavenly Kingdom. To Him be glory for ever and ever, A-men!

- 2 Timothy 4:18 N.K.J. –

I walked the lonely forest road with our two dogs. In the distance I could see a shape. Was it a bundle of rags or a living creature? The dogs walking ahead of me showed no interest. Then the shape 'sat up' and clearly visible now was a small kangaroo or young wallaby. The dogs took off! I called them but excitement deafened their obedience. I hurried on. The small creature didn't move. I prayed it would run and disappear in the scrub. But, it sat there watching with curious interest, the rapid approach of two dogs and a human. Closer and closer we came. Suddenly, a huge grey shape burst from hidden cover. A massive kangaroo (as large as a man) hopped into the centre of the road. Defiantly it looked at us.

The dogs stopped instantly. They let me put on their leads .Gently, the adult roo guided the baby off the road. In a flash they were gone.

My heart rejoiced as I remembered in that moment, the invisible Presence of our God, who brings comfort, healing and hope when we are at our weakest.

Prayer: *Thank You Lord for Your unexpected Presence when we need You. A-men.*

MEDITATIVE THOUGHT

Though invisible, His Presence is with us in us and through us, to a needing world.

Prayer for folk living in difficult and dangerous places.

REEDOM

And he who had died came out bound hand and foot with graveclothes, and his face was wrapped with a cloth. Jesus said to them "Loose him and let him go."

- John 11:44 N.K.J. –

The beautiful butterfly was trapped in the spider's web, suspended between two trees. Sunlight glistened on the colours of its franticly struggling wings. My heart ached. I decided to rescue it.

With the aid of a long stick I made increasingly high jumps swiping at the web until it finally fluttered to the ground.

It didn't fly away. It couldn't. It remained collapsed on the ground with remnants of the web and sticky residue pinning it fast. It needed to be carefully and gently cleansed and then it was free once more to live its life in flight.

Lazarus had been dead – now he was alive. He was not truly free until Jesus said "Loose him" and then the graveclothes fell away.

In Jesus Christ we have the opportunity to be 'new creations' (2 Cor:5:7) totally free from past hurts, disappointments, disillusionments, betrayals, rejections – in fact all human graveclothes and bondages. We belong to God. We are His Children and Christ has set us free to live our lives to the fullest, soaring for Him.

Prayer:

This day help us to surrender to You all that would hold us back from freely loving you and the world around us. Loose us we pray, in Jesus' Name.

MEDITATIVE THOUGHT

Prisoners actual and spiritual. Those in jails, institutions and because of faith. Folk still bound by the past.

Jesus died and rose again so that we might live spiritual lives of total freedom

GOING HOME

'For to me, to live is Christ and to die is gain'

- Phil.;v.21 –

'The cancer has returned.' My friend's voice down the phone chilled my heart.

Jean, my dear friend was loved by so many. Vibrant, funny, encourager in faith, she was a tenacious support on the committee on which we both served. She was a vital part in so many lives – loved wife, mother and grandmother and still a relatively young woman.

An army of prayer immediately surrounded her life. *'O God we uphold her into Your Keeping.'*

In the following six months we saw many miracles of Grace. With courage and faith she maintained her life. One day across the table, I **knew** she was going to die. I looked into her face and behind her smile was a glimpse of something I can only describe as 'eternal'. I was shattered. I felt led of God to pray *'Your Will be done, O Lord.'* I know many continued their prayers for her healing and I still held my faith that our God is the God of the impossible. But, something in me had shifted. My will was certainly that she would not die.

Jean went to hospital. Surrounded by her Minister, family and friends she looked into every face and said softly and calmly 'I'm going home!' The ones who came to minister to her went away having been ministered to instead.

A few days later she died. We miss her very much. Often there are tears but what a legacy, and what a testimony she has left behind. Indeed, in her life and in her death, she belonged to Jesus.

Prayer:

*Father, help us to lead surrendered lives. May we always have faith to believe You are the God of the impossible yet the courage to trust in **Your** Will for the answers we don't understand.*

A-men.

MEDITATIVE THOUGHT

All of us are journeying towards eternity.

GODLY FRIENDS LEAVE ETERNAL LEGACIES OF FAITH

DOG WITH $\mathcal{B}$ALL

When I was on holiday a few years ago, I watched a drama played out on the beach between a small dog, the unrelenting ocean waves, and the object of his passion – an old tennis ball.

The dog's owner mistimed his throwing of the ball. It soared out beyond the first couple of waves and landed right on the crest of the largest wave in the set. The ball was picked up, rolled up into the wave and then flung towards the shore. But, it was positioned so that it immediately became caught up in the outward surge to the sea and was dragged at force immediately into the path of the next creaming wave.

The little dog tried his hardest. He would swim out and be only a metre away from grabbing it back when it would be swept out of his reach. This went on for hours. Concerned people tried to distract him by giving him another ball. His owner enticed him with food treats but his eyes were on his ball and nothing else would satisfy.

This story has a surprising ending because when the tide had gone out later in the day that determined little dog found his ball again wrapped in seaweed, battered and broken but to him still the 'treasure beyond price'.

What is your greatest treasure in this life? What is the one thing you will hold on to against all the dangers and insecurities of life? What is the focus of your life? Will it stand the test of time? We all came into this life with NOTHING and as surely as the tide surges to shore each one of us is going to leave with NOTHING. There's a whole lot of 'stuff' in this world we live in. We are surrounded sometimes by 'garbage'.

What is the **most** precious thing in our lives? That's something we each individually need to think and meditate upon.

The little dog's tennis ball will fall away into dust. Possessions, money, even family and life itself will one day be gone for us as well. What is eternal? What lasts FOREVER? Should we be filling our eyes, minds and lives with the ugly and grim? Or, should we take the spiritual exhortation written long ago by St.Paul - *"Focus your lives, heart, and mind always on the things that are of beauty, holiness and good report."* Phil.4.v8 as our example of holy Truth.

I thank God in my times of meditation for faith that strengthens me though all the wild seas of life and for Jesus Christ who shows me still by His Spirit, the way to a life of Hope, Happiness and Peace amongst a world of disarray. **Something to meditate and think about**. What is our focus? What is our greatest treasure?

The dog's greatest treasure was his ball.

ℛEFLECTIONS

Read 2 Cor. 3:18

Christ in you; the hope of Glory

- Colossians 2:27b (N.K.J.) -

I stood on the deck of the cruise boat and the reflections from the bank were beautiful. The churning wake caused by the engines disturbed the water near the vessel.

Suddenly, the light shifted or a breeze blew – a perfect image came. With my simple camera I clicked, and the picture taken is inspirational. When the sky and clouds of heaven covered the turmoil of the river it produced stillness and perfect peace.

We are **all** called to be 'as Christ' in this broken world. We also are being changed into His Image. We can then bring to others a touch of God's Divine Love and make a difference.

Prayer: Dear Lord Jesus,

Help us to follow You as Shepherd, in Word and Spirit, to bring change in the lives of others. In Your Holy Name…a-men.

PRAYER FOCUS: All whose lives are in turmoil

THOUGHT FOR THE DAY:

Our relationship with Christ should be reflected to others.

FRAGRANT SHOCK

Read 2 Cor 2: 14 –17

We are to God the fragrance of Christ among those who are being saved and among those who are perishing.

- 2 Cor 2:15 N.K.J. -

My home is in a small rural area. One of my problems is field mice. They sometimes come inside onto the pantry shelves.

I was horrified when I took out a special tray to take to a function. It was covered with what looked like mouse droppings. Carefully I carried it to an open window. A gentle breeze and my movement disturbed the 'droppings'.

A beautiful fragrance wafted through the house. Apparently, a jar of dried rosemary leaves had fallen over and spilled from the shelf above. The perfume from this scattered herb changed the atmosphere.

If our lives are filled with the fragrance of Christ's Presence in us we should be the same kind of shock to an unbelieving world. What a wonderful thought!

Thought for the Day

Is the fragrance of Christ evident in my life this day?

Prayer:

Lord help us to draw closer to You. May we bring your Love and Fragrance to a darkening world. We remember folks in remote areas whose daily problems may be different to ours. A-men.

EMPTED

Read: 1 Cor: 11 - 12,13

He leads me in the paths of righteousness for His name's sake.

- Psalm. 23:3b (NKJ) -

The supermarket aisles were jammed. People jostled to be processed and released on their way. I was being helped with the unloading of my trolley. As the total came up on the checkout screen I noticed a black plastic square on the bottom of the trolley.

'I don't remember that being there before.' I was being hurried along when another thought came. *Where's your meat?* Then I knew. The upturned plastic was an overturned small tray of very expensive steak. *You're going to hold everyone up. Think of the savings! No one will know. It's not your fault.*

I had to make an instant decision.

"I'm sorry but something has been missed." I heard the loud groans. 'It's that older lady who's holding us up.' My order was repriced and I left. As I walked away from the mutterings and shopping tensions, I was aware of an incredible sense of peace and well-being.

This life is full of major temptations. Only Christ can give us the Strength to triumph even in the 'little' ones.

Prayer: Dear Lord, Keep our hearts **pure** before You. In the 'little' things as well as 'major' choices be our Guide and Strength this day.

In Jesus' Name a-men.

Thought for the Day: People around as well as God see and know the choices we make.

Prayer Focus: Folks tempted by adverse circumstances to compromise on their integrity.

A thought: The Pathway of integrity is not always clear but the **PEACE** it brings is beyond price or adequate description.

ROCK OF REDEMPTION

Read John 8: 4-11

He who is without sin among you, let him throw a stone at her first.

- John 8:7 (N.K.J.) –

A verse of a famous hymn "Will your anchor hold?" by Pricilla Jane Owens inspires with the words:

> *We have an anchor that keeps the soul*
> *Steadfast and sure while the billows roll;*
> *Fastened to the rock which cannot move,*
> *Grounded firm and deep in the Saviour's Love*

In the story of the woman caught in adultery (John Chapter 8) the only sinless person present was the Lord Himself. Instead of casting a stone he reached out with compassion, forgiveness and Divine Love.

On the cross at Calvary this sinless one was then crushed (Isaiah 54-5) as the weight of a sinful world fell like a rock of judgment upon Him.

What a wonderful image we can now have of the workings of an awesome God. The Holy One ground down, rises from the grave - a huge rock of restraint is thrown aside. He becomes **the** Rock of divine Love – Hope for eternity to all who follow Him.

Prayer: Dear Lord, thank You. Help us to live lives worthy of Your sacrifice and amazing Love. a-men

Prayer Focus: Those who still don't know the Saviour's forgiveness and love.

THOUGHT: Our sometimes heavy, rock-like burdens – Jesus lifts and shares.

ROCK EVOCATIVE OF STABILITY

A LIFE ANCHORED TO *H*IM WILL HOLD

STRONG, CALM SANITY

Read: Romans 8, Galatians 2:20

It is no longer I who live but Christ who lives in me.

- Galatians 2:20(b) -

News of disasters flood the airways. Deception and lies wage war with Truth in many areas of our society. Sometimes even our lives can resemble a whirlpool with swirling issues of family, finances, and various other needs.

Oswald Chambers' life was short. He died tragically and unexpectedly in 1917 at age 43. Yet, he left an incredible legacy of inspired writing which resonate with holy Truth in our modern world. In his book *My Utmost for His Highest*, he wrote: **Strong, calm sanity – the outworking of an intimate relationship with a living God.**

This is certainly a Truth to me. Through sorrow, illness and life changes knowing the certainty of Jesus Christ as Saviour/Lord who lives in us (Col 1:29) made it possible to maintain a connection with a Divine God through all the journeying of life. This is a gift for **all** who follow Him.

Because Christ lives we **all** can face our tomorrows with confidence.

Prayer: Thank You Lord for the Strength you give us to live with calm sanity amid life's storms. A-men.

Prayer: For outpouring of Comfort and Divine Love on the lives of those who grieve.

Thought: We may be 'Peculiar' people in the eyes of the world but in God's eyes are being 'perfected' into Christ's sane image.

Ripples on the surface
but STRONG, CALM SANITY brings HOLY PEACE

Read: Ezekiel 37: 1-14 - *Vision of Dry Bones*

I have come that they may have life, and that they may have it more abundantly.

- John 10.10b N.K.J. -

The small frog was stiff. There was no sign of life. I felt sad. Its body had been wedged under the lid of the upright freezer in the laundry. It had wriggled beneath and been unable to back out because of the cold.

I carried it gently outside to bury in the garden. In the warmth of my hand one tiny leg began to quiver. I gently rubbed it. Gradually one leg at a time began to move. I placed it on a rock in the sun and watched with great joy as it later hopped away seemingly full of energy and life.

The story of the Prophet Ezekiel and the dry bones reminds us that spiritually we KNOW our God can and forever will exercise His sovereign acts in life's circumstances. Nothing for Him is impossible.

Jesus' commandment to us John 15:12 *'Love one another as I have loved you'*, means in our normal lives we are to love, care, nurture and bring life and Divine Hope to folks around us. Perhaps He will call us also to pray the breath of God's Spirit and Life on even ones seemingly frozen in their circumstances.

Prayer: Beloved Lord, Lead us always to be Your Hands, Your Heart, Your Life of nurture, to all the people around. In Jesus' Name a-men.

Prayer Focus: Carers everywhere, homes, hospitals, nursing homes.

Thought for the Day:

The simple touch of a hand and a kind word can transform the life of another.

Prayer Focus: Carers everywhere, homes, hospitals, nursing homes.

Thought for the Day:

The simple touch of a hand and a kind word can transform the life of another.

The possibilities of God are often unclear.
Faith and loving care are our responsibility.

PEACE

God's peace is not about absence of trouble and strife.

Thought to ponder:

Inner Peace enables us to feed our souls with images we have stored in our minds. These may be of journeying in a small boat across the seas, or a time or place where our hearts were touched by beauty. This inner place is where GOD can then, through HIS Holy and Still Presence, pour His Oil of Healing onto the troubled waters of life's circumstances.

This leads to conversation – Prayer – a two-way 'connection'

All Meditations in this book have previously been published by Upper Room a morning Devotional.

I give grateful thanks to the editors and producers of The Upper Room for their encouragement and support for meas I desired to write addressing life themes in alignment with Scripture verses.

www.ingramcontent.com/pod-product-compliance
Lightning Source LLC
Chambersburg PA
CBRC090825120626
46547CB00007B/606